IF I WERE BIGGER THAN ANYONE
And Other Poems

Illustrated by
Clara Vulliamy

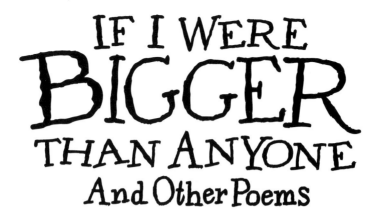

WALKER BOOKS
AND SUBSIDIARIES

LONDON • BOSTON • SYDNEY

HICKORY, DICKORY, DOCK

Hickory, dickory, dock,
The mouse ran up the clock.
The clock struck one,
The mouse ran down,
Hickory, dickory, dock.

WEE WILLIE WINKIE

Wee Willie Winkie
runs through the town,
Upstairs and downstairs
in his night-gown,
Rapping at the window,
crying through the lock,
Are the children all in bed,
for now it's eight o'clock?

Maths Together

There's a lot more to maths than numbers and sums;
it's an important language which helps us describe, explore and
explain the world we live in. So the earlier children develop
an appreciation and understanding of maths, the better.

We use maths all the time – when we shop or travel from one
place to another, for example. Even when we fill the kettle we are
estimating and judging quantities. Many games and puzzles
involve maths. So too do stories and poems, often
in an imaginative and interesting way.

Maths Together is a collection of high-quality picture
books designed to introduce children, simply and enjoyably, to
basic mathematical ideas – from counting and measuring to pattern
and probability. By listening to the stories and rhymes, talking about
them and asking questions, children will gain the confidence to
try out the mathematical ideas for themselves – an
important step in their numeracy development.

You don't have to be a mathematician to help your child
learn maths. Just as by reading aloud you play a vital role in their
literacy development, so by sharing the *Maths Together* books
with your child, you will play an important part in developing their
understanding of mathematics. To help you, each book has detailed
notes at the back, explaining the mathematical ideas that it
introduces, with suggestions for further related activities.

With *Maths Together*, you can count on doing the
very best for your child.

For Caroline
C.V.

First published 1999 by Walker Books Ltd
87 Vauxhall Walk, London SE11 5HJ

2 4 6 8 10 9 7 5 3 1
This selection © 1999 Walker Books
Illustrations © 1999 Clara Vulliamy
Introductory and concluding notes © 1999 Jeannie Billington and Grace Cook

This book has been typeset in Century Old Style.
Printed in Singapore

British Library Cataloguing in Publication Data
A catalogue record for this book is available from the British Library.

ISBN 0-7445-6829-3 (hb)
ISBN 0-7445-6821-8 (pb)

PUSSY IN DE MOONLIGHT

Pussy in de moonlight
Pussy in de zoo
Pussy never come home
Till half past two.

I HAVE A LITTLE CHIMING CLOCK

I have a little chiming clock,
I love to hear it ring.
Every day at one o'clock
It ... goes ... TING!

I have a little chiming clock,
I love to hear it ring.
Every day at two o'clock
It ... goes ... TING! TING!

etc.

TOASTER TIME

Tick tick tick tick tick tick tick
Toast up a sandwich quick quick quick
Hamwich
Or jamwich
Lick lick lick!

Tick tick tick tick tick tick – stop!
POP!

Eve Merriam

WHAT THE GIANT HAD FOR DINNER

First
He ate
A hive of bees.

Next
He ate
Some chestnut trees.

Then
He ate
A house near me.

Last
Of all
He drank the sea.

Ian McMillan and Martyn Wiley

BEFORE THE BATH

It's cold, cold, cold,
And the water shines wet,
And the longer I wait
The colder I get.

I can't quite make
Myself hop in
All shivery-cold
In just my skin.

Yet the water's warm
In the tub, I know.
So – one, two, three,
And IN I go!

Corinna Marsh

AFTER MY BATH

After my bath
I try, try, try
to wipe myself
till I'm dry, dry, dry.

Hands to wipe
and fingers and toes
and two wet legs
and a shiny nose.

Just think how much
less time I'd take
if I were a dog
and could shake, shake, shake.

Aileen Fisher

REMEMBER

Remember when
the world was tall
and you were small
and legs were all
you saw?

Thin legs
fat legs
dog legs
cat legs.

Table legs
chair legs
dark legs
fair legs.

Quick legs
slow legs
nowhere-
to-go legs.

Jumping legs
prancing legs
skipping legs
dancing legs.

Shoes-and-sock legs
on-the-rocks legs.

Standing-very-tall legs
running-all-around legs.

Stooping-very-small legs
lying-on-the-ground legs.

Remember when
the world was tall
and you were small
and legs were all
you saw?

Pamela Mordecai

IF I WERE
BIGGER THAN ANYONE

If I were bigger than anyone,
 If I were taller than trees,
I could step over hills and towns
 And go anywhere I pleased.

If I got bored with being huge,
 The next day I'd be small.
 But the size I really am
 I might not choose at all.

Ruth Harnden

BAA, BAA, BLACK SHEEP

Baa, baa, black sheep,
Have you any wool?
Yes sir, yes sir,
Three bags full:
One for the master,
And one for the dame,
And one for the little boy
Who lives down the lane.

HALFWAY DOWN

Halfway down the stairs
Is a stair
Where I sit.
There isn't any
Other stair
Quite like
It.
I'm not at the bottom,
I'm not at the top;
So this is the stair
Where
I always
Stop.

Halfway up the stairs
Isn't up,
And isn't down.
It isn't in the nursery,
It isn't in the town.
And all sorts of funny thoughts
Run round my head:
"It isn't really
Anywhere!
It's somewhere else
Instead!"

A A Milne

FIVE LITTLE FROGGIES

Five little froggies sitting on a well;
One looked up and down he fell;
Froggies jumped high
Froggies jumped low;
Four little froggies dancing to and fro.

Four little froggies sitting on a well…

etc.

JUST WATCH

Watch
how high
I'm jumping,

Watch
how far
I hop,

Watch
how long
I'm skipping,

Watch
how fast
I stop!

**Myra
Cohn Livingston**

MY SISTER LAURA

My sister Laura's bigger than me
And lifts me up quite easily.
I can't lift her, I've tried and tried;
She must have something heavy inside.

Spike Milligan

ONE ELEPHANT

One elephant went out to play
Upon a spider's web one day.
He thought it such a tremendous stunt
That he called for another little elephant.

Two elephants went out to play
Upon a spider's web one day.
They thought it such a tremendous stunt
That they called for another little elephant.

Three elephants went out to play
Upon a spider's web one day.
The web went CREAK
The web went CRACK
And all of a sudden
They all ran back.

YELLOW BUTTER

Yellow butter purple jelly red jam black bread

Spread it thick
Say it quick

Yellow butter purple jelly red jam black bread

Spread it thicker
Say it quicker

Yellow butter purple jelly red jam black bread

Now repeat it
While you eat it

Yellow butter purple jelly red jam black bread

Don't talk
With your mouth full!

Mary Ann Hoberman

MIX A PANCAKE

Mix a pancake,
Stir a pancake,
Pop it in the pan;
Fry the pancake,
Toss the pancake –
Catch it if you can.

Christina Rossetti

TOOTHSOME

No need to squeeze out half a tube
Of toothpaste, honeybunch –
Unless you plan to use it in
A sandwich for your lunch?

Norah Smaridge

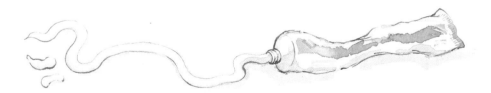

About this book

All of the poems in *If I Were Bigger Than Anyone*
are about different kinds of measuring.

"Remember", "If I Were Bigger Than Anyone", "Five Little Froggies"
and "Halfway Down" are all about measuring
height and length. "My Sister Laura" and "One Elephant" are
about weighing. "Baa, Baa, Black Sheep" is about volume.
"Yellow Butter", "Mix a Pancake" and "Toothsome" are all about
surface area. "Before the Bath" is about temperature.

Children find measuring time particularly hard.
"Hickory, Dickory, Dock", "Wee Willie Winkie", "Pussy in de Moonlight"
and "I Have a Little Chiming Clock" are all about telling the time.
Other poems are more general: "Toaster Time" and "After My Bath"
are about the passing of time, "What the Giant Had for Dinner",
which uses words like *first*, *next*, *then* and *last*, is about the
order of time.

In most of the poems, making comparisons is the starting
point for measurement. Some of the poems use standard units
of measurement: "Hickory, Dickory, Dock", for instance, measures
time in hours. Others, like "Just Watch", provide an
opportunity for you and your child to discuss other,
less precise ways of measuring.

Throughout the book there are lots of measuring words –
full, *halfway*, *big*, *heavy*, *thick*, and so on –
which your child will become familiar with.

Notes for parents

The first four poems in the book are about telling the time. As you read them, look at the times on the clocks in the pictures. You can point out other clocks in the home and street, some of which may be digital.

Froggies jumped high...

When the little hand is on the 1 and the big hand is at the top, it's one o'clock.

Some of the poems, like "Five Little Froggies", "Just Watch" and "Mix a Pancake", encourage children to join in with actions. Taking part helps them to understand the measuring words better.

Yes, you could. He's lighter than you.

I could lift Jake up.

Children love making comparisons, particularly in relation to themselves. Many of the poems compare one thing with another, encouraging you and your child to do the same.

We are measuring all the time, for example when we think about how far, how heavy, or how much things hold. All sorts of everyday activities give you the chance to talk about measuring.

I'll get the towel.

Will you be high enough on that box?

When children play in the bath and sandpit they can see how much water and sand different containers hold. They can also see how water rises in a cup when they put an object in it.

Counting down to a special event is a wonderful way to measure the passing of time. You could make a row of objects to show the number of days left, and take one away each morning, or cross the days off a calendar instead.

Gran

Only three more days till Gran comes.

Your child can learn a lot from watching you measuring things in the kitchen. They will have fun helping, too!

I need two cups of rice. Can you fill the cup?

Children enjoy cutting shapes from rolled-out pastry or playdough. They can try to cut out as many shapes as possible.

Will my star fit?

Maths Together

The *Maths Together* programme is divided into two sets –
yellow (age 3+) and green (age 5+). There are six books in
each set, helping children learn maths through story,
rhyme, games and puzzles.